A Splash of Fear

by Jo Cotterill
Illustrated by Ana Sebastian

OXFORD

UNIVERSITY PRESS

Chapter 1
The invitation

George ran across the playground. "Dad, guess what I've got?" he said, reaching into his pocket. George produced an envelope. "It's a party invitation from Sanjeev!"

His dad gave him a hug. "You only started at this school last week! An invitation already? That's great!"

'Produce' means to bring something out to show people, or to make something. When George produced the envelope, does this mean he made it or that he took it out of his pocket?

Back at home, Dad read the invitation carefully. "The party is next month at the leisure centre. It's a pool party."

George frowned in response. "A pool party?"

"You know, where the person having the party hires the swimming pool just for them and their friends," Dad explained.

George frowned in response at the idea of a pool party. How else could George have responded? How would you respond if you were invited to a pool party?

George's throat felt tight. "But, Dad, you know I can't swim very well," he said. "What if I'm the only one at the party who can't really swim?"

"Don't worry," Dad said, giving him a warm smile. "I doubt you'll be the only one, but we'll go to the pool at the weekend and get some practice in."

Chapter 2
Splash!

The glass doors slid open, and George and his dad walked into the leisure centre.

George stared through the huge window into the swimming pool. There were lots of people in the water, all splashing around happily.

"Surely I'm going to enjoy this," George said to himself, as his dad went to pay at the desk.

George told himself that he was surely going to enjoy swimming. How do *you* think he felt at this moment?

In the changing room, George's tummy felt funny, almost like it had its own swimming pool inside it.

"Excited?" asked Dad, as he put their things in a locker.

"Sort of," replied George.

As they walked out of the changing room, the shouts and splashes of the people in the water echoed around the walls.

"I'll go down the steps first, and then I'll help you in," Dad said. Once he was in the water, he offered George his hand. "You can do it. Just take it slowly."

George's legs felt wobbly as he put one foot then the other into the warm water. He began to climb down the steps, holding Dad's hand, which felt solid and firm. Before he knew it, he had reached the bottom step. The water came up to his waist.

"There you go!" said Dad, <u>satisfied</u>.

George felt a surge of pride and relief. He splashed Dad and giggled. Dad splashed back. It was just like being in a big bath!

If you are <u>satisfied</u>, you are pleased or happy with a situation. Why do you think George's dad was <u>satisfied</u> here?

Another boy jumped in from the side. *Splash!*

"I want to do that!" George exclaimed. He waded back to the steps, climbed up and walked along the side of the pool. Excitement tickled his tummy.

He took a breath, lifted his arms, stepped forwards and jumped.

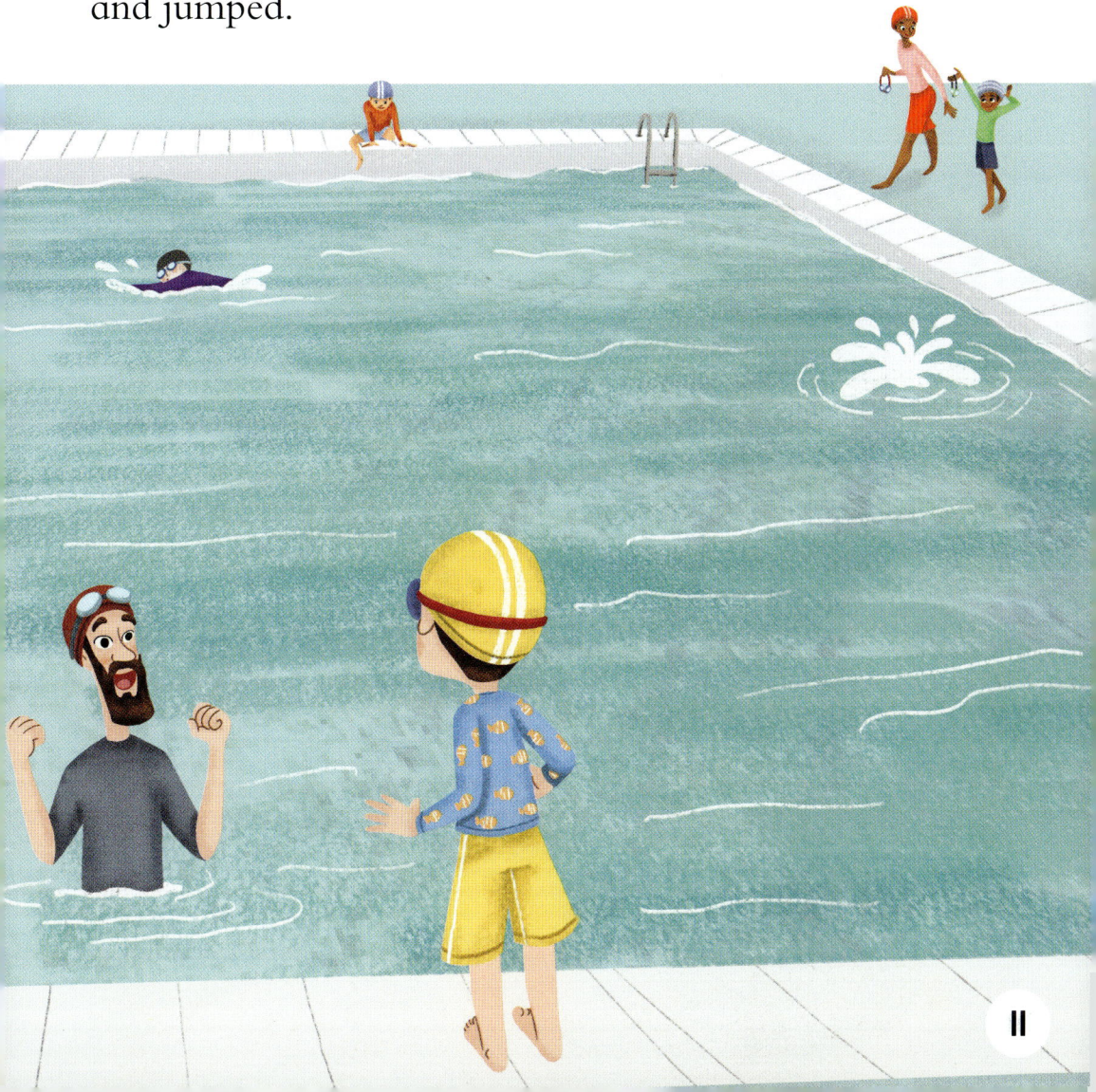

Chapter 3
Reaching the bottom

George sank quickly. He reached for the bottom of the pool with his feet. Where was it? He couldn't feel anything solid. The water closed over his head, and George began to panic. He needed to breathe. He thrashed his arms and legs wildly.

Then a hand reached down and pulled him up.
As soon as his head was out of the water, George
took a huge gulp of air.

"It's OK, George," Dad said gently. "You're OK."

George's foot struck the bottom of the pool. He stood up, shakily. The water only came up to his chest. "I want to get out," he said, trembling.

"George, it's OK," said Dad.

"No!" said George. "I'm getting out!"

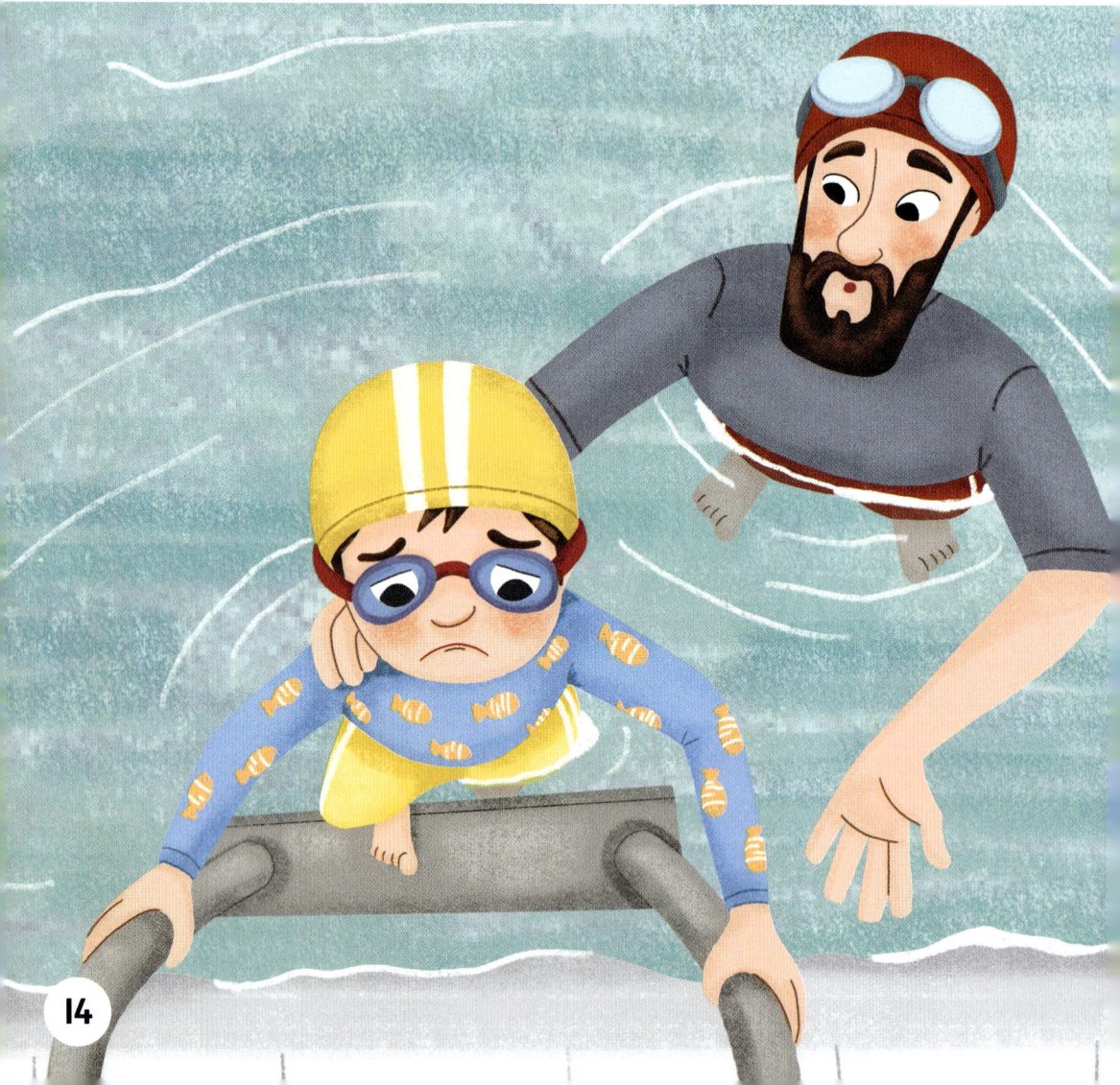

George couldn't stop shaking, even after he'd got dressed again.

Dad tried to help. "It was just a shock, George. You weren't in any danger."

It hadn't felt like that to George.

"You'll be fine at the pool party," Dad said.

"I'm not going to the party!" snapped George.

Chapter 4
Fighting fear

The next day, George's classmates talked a lot about the pool party.

Sanjeev was very excited. "They're going to get out all the floats for us!" he said.

Penny, the girl who sat next to George in class, turned to him. "Are you coming?" she asked.

George mumbled a response and looked away. He felt <u>miserable</u>. He wanted to make friends at this new school, but he couldn't admit he was scared of going in the water.

Why did George feel <u>miserable</u>? Can you think of another word to describe how George was feeling?

After school, Dad took George to the playground. "What are you going to do about the pool party?" Dad asked, as he watched George push himself back and forth on the swing.

"Nothing. I don't know," said George grumpily. "I don't want to talk about it."

For the next three days, Dad said nothing about swimming. Then on Saturday, over breakfast, he suddenly said, "Did you know that when I was your age, I was scared of going in the water?"

George looked at him in surprise. "Really? Why?"

"I fell out of a boat," Dad said in response. "Your grandad loved fishing. He took me out with him on his boat at weekends. It was amazing, being on the water. One day, I leaned out too far over the side and fell in the water."

Dad took a sip of tea. "Even though I was wearing a life jacket, I was scared," he said. "The water went in my mouth – it tasted horrible! Grandad quickly rescued me, but I didn't want to go anywhere near a lake or a swimming pool again."

"You can swim now, though," said George.

"I had lessons," Dad explained. "They helped give me confidence in the water." He hesitated for a moment. "I could <u>arrange</u> some lessons for you, if you like?"

Dad offered to <u>arrange</u> some swimming lessons for George. Does this mean that Dad will book some lessons for George, or that they will go along to the pool and hope he can have a lesson?

George was about to refuse. Then he thought about the pool party and the floats, and about Sanjeev and Penny and the others at school. Surely a swimming lesson would help him feel better about the party? He really did want to go. So …

"All right," he said. "I'll try *one* lesson."

Chapter 5
Learning to swim

There were four other children in the swimming lesson with George.

"Hello," said the teacher, smiling at them. "My name is Sarah. I know you're all probably a bit nervous, so we're just going to sit on the side with our legs in the water for now."

George felt relieved. Sit on the side? That wasn't scary at all!

The five of them sat down and kicked their legs in the water.

"Now, splash me as hard as you can!" Sarah said.
George thought splashing Sarah was lots of fun!
Then Sarah helped them into the water, and they
practised walking sideways, like crabs.

"Good!" the teacher said. "Now how about holding on to the side and kicking your legs?"

There was a lot of splashing and a lot of giggling. Then Sarah got a small plastic watering can and 'watered' their heads. They had to pretend they were seeds. "These seeds will <u>produce</u> great swimmers!" she said.

What does Sarah mean when she says the "seeds will <u>produce</u> great swimmers"? Can you think of another word to use instead of '<u>produce</u>'?

George had so much fun, he forgot all about being scared. "Can I come back next week?" he asked Dad.

"Of course you can," said Dad with a smile. "Before long, you'll be a champion swimmer."

Chapter 6
Pool party!

It was the day of the party. The pool was full of George's classmates, yelling and splashing and having fun.

George noticed Penny was standing on the side of the pool by herself, looking miserable. "Are you OK?" he asked.

"I'm not very good at swimming," Penny confessed. "I shouldn't have come. I can't go in the water. What if I sink?"

George smiled kindly. "It's not as scary as you think. Sit on the side with me and kick your legs in the water."

"You're a good teacher," Penny said later, as George showed her how to walk across the pool sideways.

"I'll tell you a secret," said George. "I was afraid of the water too. Then my dad arranged for me to have swimming lessons, and now I love it."

"Swimming lessons?" asked Penny. "Do you think I could have some too?"

"I'm sure you could if your mum agrees," George said. "You could join my class!"

"Thanks, George," said Penny with a smile. "You're a good friend."

George grinned back. "Now, let's find a watering can!"

Read and discuss

Read and talk about the following questions.

Page 2: Can you pretend to open an envelope and produce an invitation?

Page 3: George says, "A pool party?" in response to the invitation. Can you say George's response to Dad in different ways, for example as if you were bored or excited?

Page 6: Have you been anywhere that you thought surely would be different to how it actually was, for example a new school or activity club?

Page 10: Can you think of a time when you felt satisfied with something you had done?

Page 17: Can you show what George's face looked like when he felt miserable?

Page 22: George's dad arranged some swimming lessons for him. Do you do any activities that are arranged for you at school or at home?